APR 2 6 2017

Money and Trade in Our World

Shelly Buchanan, M.S.Ed.

Consultants

Shelley Scudder
Gifted Education Teacher
Broward County Schools

Caryn Williams, M.S.Ed.
Madison County Schools
Huntsville, AL

Publishing Credits

Conni Medina, *M.A.Ed., Managing Editor*
Lee Aucoin, *Creative Director*
Torrey Maloof, *Editor*
Marissa Rodriguez, *Designer*
Stephanie Reid, *Photo Editor*
Rachelle Cracchiolo, *M.S.Ed., Publisher*

Image Credits: Cover, pp.1, 23 Alamy;
p.19 Associated Press; pp.22, 28,
29 (top right) Getty Images; p.29
(left center) iStockphoto; p.6 The
Library of Congress [LC-USF33-
030642-M4]; p.8 The Library of
Congress [LC-RG15-B41-12]; p.15
The Library of Congress [LC-DIG-
matpc-19737]; p.24 The Library of
Congress [LC-USZ62-84467]; p.4 North
Wind Picture Archives; p.13 REUTERS/
Newscom; All other images from
Shutterstock.

Teacher Created Materials
5301 Oceanus Drive
Huntington Beach, CA 92649-1030
http://www.tcmpub.com
ISBN 978-1-4333-7002-1
© 2014 Teacher Created Materials, Inc.

Table of Contents

Arabia

Africa

These traders are on the Silk Road in Asia.

Traders from Long Ago

People have been buying and selling things for thousands of years. Long ago, **traders** traveled many miles. Some rode on camels. Others sailed on ships.

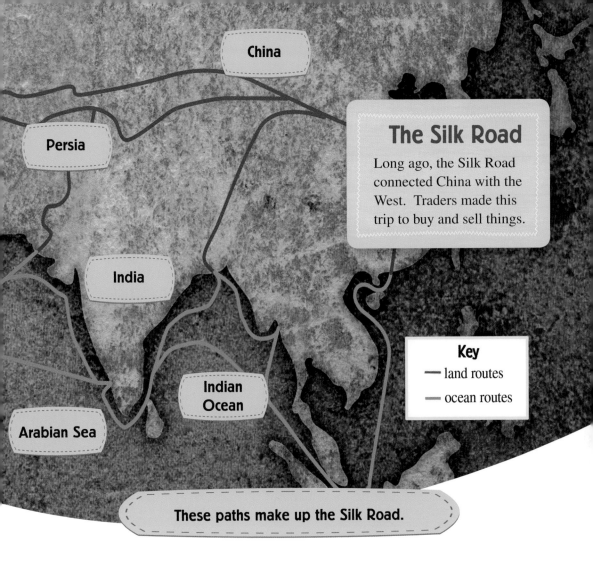

China

Persia

The Silk Road

Long ago, the Silk Road connected China with the West. Traders made this trip to buy and sell things.

India

Key
— land routes
— ocean routes

Indian
Ocean

Arabian Sea

These paths make up the Silk Road.

It took months to reach the markets. There, the traders would buy and sell things such as silk and spices. Silk is a smooth material used to make clothes. People use spices to add flavor to food.

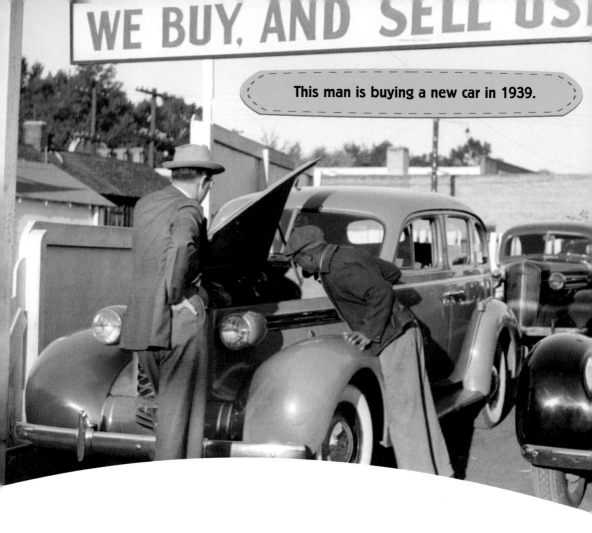

WE BUY, AND SELL US[...]

This man is buying a new car in 1939.

Goods and Services

People from around the world still trade goods with one another. Goods are things that can be bought and sold.

This boy is buying goods in India.

You can touch and hold goods. Books and food are goods. Clothes and cars are goods, too.

People also trade services. A *service* is work or help that is for sale. It is a job that one person does for another person.

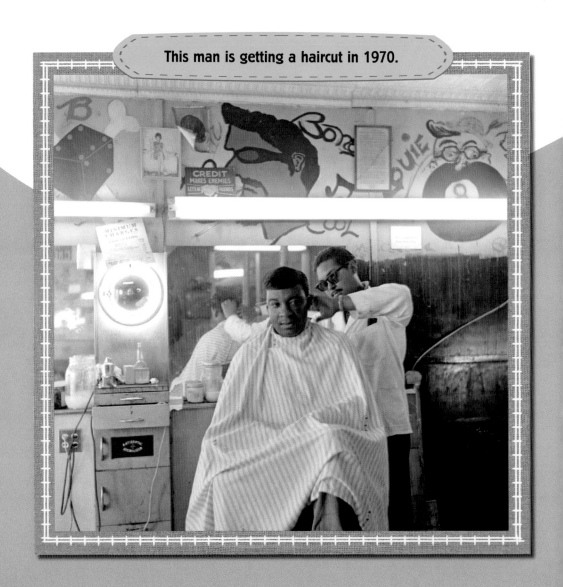

This man is getting a haircut in 1970.

If you are sick, you go see a doctor. A doctor provides a service. Fixing a car is a service, too. So is giving a haircut.

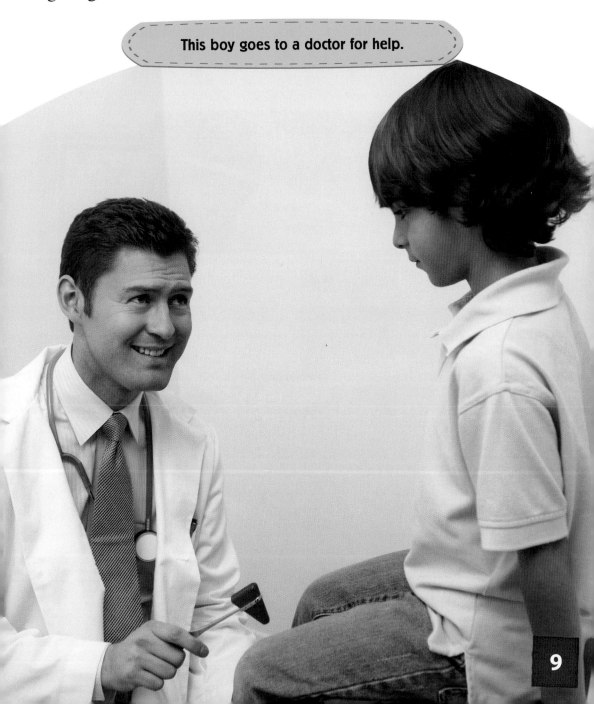

This boy goes to a doctor for help.

Trade Today

Long ago, trade was slow. It took a long time for goods to move from one place to another. Trade happens much faster now.

This airplane carries goods.

Today, ships carry **containers** filled with goods. They can cross the sea in a week. An airplane can make the trip in just a few hours. Trucks drive goods quickly from town to town. Things move fast!

This ship carries many containers.

Today, we are linked to people all around the world. One country can **produce**, or make, goods that other countries need. The United States produces things such as food and airplanes.

This airplane is being built in the United States.

Other countries produce goods that the United States needs. They produce things like oil and coffee. Countries depend on each other to get what they need.

This man works at an oil plant in the Persian Gulf.

These are coffee beans.

Resources

Each country has special goods it sells to other countries. Workers use **natural resources** (REE-sohrs-ez) from their country to make these goods. Natural resources are found in nature.

Wind Power

Wind is a natural resource. Wind turbines (TUR-baynz) turn the wind's energy into power we can use.

These are wind turbines.

14

Natural resources include wood, stone, oil, and wind. People make goods from these resources. People in other countries can buy these goods.

These men are cutting down trees to make boards in 1934.

There are also **human resources**. These are people with special **skills**. They do the work. Teachers and doctors are human resources.

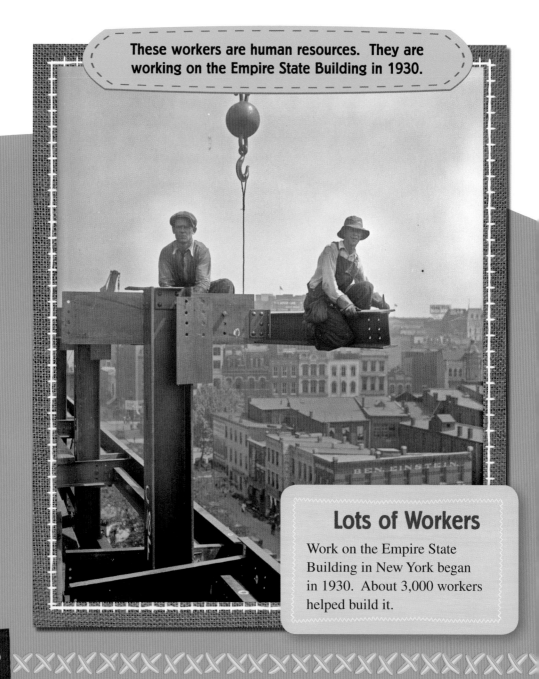

These workers are human resources. They are working on the Empire State Building in 1930.

Lots of Workers

Work on the Empire State Building in New York began in 1930. About 3,000 workers helped build it.

Capital resources are goods used to make other goods. Tools are capital resources. For example, a hammer helps a worker build a house.

This man uses tools to build an airplane.

The Ins and Outs

Goods that come into one country from another country are called **imports**. Can you think of some imports? Look at the labels on some items in your home. Many will say where the goods were made.

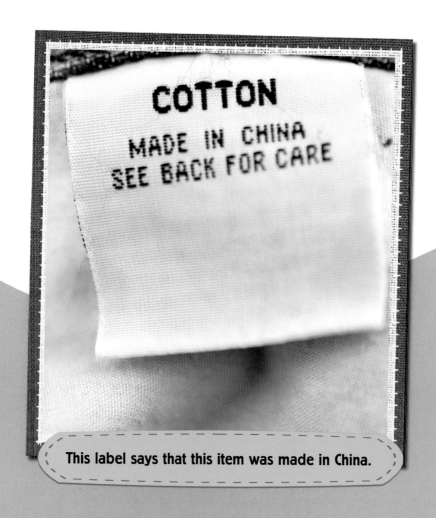

This label says that this item was made in China.

Japan produces many cars. China produces clothing. Mexico is known for its fruit.

This woman makes cars in Japan.

In Canada, people use these bins to collect maple syrup from maple trees.

Exports are goods that one country sends to another country to sell. What a country exports depends on its natural resources.

This man is drying coffee beans in Brazil.

Many maple trees grow in Canada. So, Canada exports the most maple syrup in the world. The weather in Brazil is good for coffee plants. So, Brazil exports the most coffee.

Money Matters

People buy things with **currency** (KUR-uhn-see), or money. Many countries have their own currency. In the United States, you pay for goods with dollars.

These boys buy pencils using dollars.

In Mexico, you buy things with pesos (PEY-sohs). In Japan, you pay in yen. There are more than 140 currencies in the world!

This girl is holding pesos.

Making Choices

When you buy something, you make a choice. This choice you make affects people around the world. This is because we are all linked together through trade.

Wants and Needs

Sometimes, you buy something you want, such as a book. Other times, you buy something you need, such as food.

This boy buys a wagon he wants in 1937.

If you buy a game made in Japan, you help the people who made the game. They get some of the money you paid for the game.

This boy plays a video game made in Japan.

You are part of trade! You buy things, or your family buys things for you. You use money. You use goods made in other countries.

This girl is shopping for clothes that are made in other countries.

What you and your family buy makes a difference around the world. Your choices matter.

This boy uses money to buy a toy he wants.

Count It!

Many goods in your home or school were made in other countries. These might be clothes, toys, and food. Look at the labels on the things you find. Where did they come from? Count the number of countries you find.

This olive oil is made in Greece.

This computer is made in China.

AAA R03X2 MADE IN CHINA
QUIV

This shirt is made in India.

100%
PURE WOOL
MADE IN INDIA

MADE IN JAPAN
日本国　長野制造

This bowl is made in Japan.

Glossary

capital resources—goods used by people to make other goods

containers—large boxes that goods are placed in so they can be moved on ships, trucks, airplanes, or trains

currency—the money that a country uses

exports—goods sent out of the country for sale

human resources—people with skills who do the work

imports—goods brought into the country for sale

natural resources—materials found in nature such as water or wood

produce—to make

skills—abilities that people have

traders—people who buy, sell, or trade goods

Index

Your Turn!

Your Choices Matter

This boy is playing a video game. The game was made in China. Think of the last thing you or your parents bought. Where was it made? What people do you think were affected by your choice?